THE HERMITAGE

Selected Treasures from One of the World's
Great Museums

THE HERMITAGE

Selected Treasures from One of the World's
Great Museums

Text written by the curatorial staff of The State Hermitage Museum
Commissioned by The Hermitage Joint Venture

DOUBLEDAY
New York London Toronto Sydney Auckland

PUBLISHED BY DOUBLEDAY
a division of Bantam Doubleday Dell Publishing Group, Inc.
666 Fifth Avenue, New York, New York 10103

DOUBLEDAY and the portrayal of an anchor
with a dolphin are trademarks of Doubleday,
a division of Bantam Doubleday Dell Publishing Group, Inc.

Produced by Booth-Clibborn Editions, Inc., for The Hermitage Joint Venture

Editor
Edward Booth-Clibborn

Assistant Editor
Denny Hemming

Designer
David Hillman
Pentagram Design Limited

Photographers
Vladimir Terebenin
Leonard Haifets

Translators
Jan Butler
Katharine Judelson

Plan Illustration
Stephen Gyapay

Library of Congress Cataloging-in-Publication Data

The Hermitage: selected treasures from one of the world's great
        museums/text written by the curatorial staff of The State Hermitage
        Museum: commissioned by The Hermitage Joint Venture. – 1st ed. in
        the U.S.
            p.   cm.
        Includes index.
        1. Art–Russian S.FS.R.–Leningrad–Catalogs. 2. Gosudarstvenny ï
Érmitazh (Soviet Union)–Catalogs.   I. Gosudarstvenny ï Érmitazh
(Soviet Union)
N3350.H48   1991   91-224
708.7'453–dc20   CIP

ISBN 0-385-41966-X

Printed by Dai Nippon, Japan
June 1991
First Edition in the United States of America

Contents

Introduction

Far Left
The Portico of the New Hermitage (Built by the architects Leo von Klenze, Vasily Stasov and Nikolai Yefimov; sculptures by Alexander Terebenev; 1839-51)

St Petersburg, known today as Leningrad, was the capital of the Russian Empire for more than 200 years. During that period the city came to embody the spirit of Russia in its palaces, its architecture, its flourishing trade and in the organization of its day-to-day life. It was built to a comprehensive plan conceived by Peter the Great himself. Hence the stylistic unity of the city's architecture and the strikingly original composition of the townscape as a series of architectural ensembles. The growth of the city was largely determined by its geographical position and its topography for it embraces more than 100 islands, linked by over 300 bridges, thus rightly deserving its name 'Venice of the North'. The city is divided into two parts by its main artery, the river Neva, which provides the focal point of the architectural concept.

European culture has also played an integral part in shaping the appearance of the city. Throughout history, Russia has maintained close links with the cultural traditions of Europe, and from the sixteenth century onwards foreign architects and artists were invited to her cities. Under Peter the Great this practice was encouraged more than ever before, since not only local craftsmen but also artistic skills from abroad were in great demand in what was the new capital of an enormous empire. Throughout the eighteenth century this trend continued, reflecting the concerns of Russia's Age of Reason, or Age of Enlightenment, which effected a wave of new reforms that involved all aspects of Russian life.

The Hermitage, created by Catherine the Great with the aid of her distinguished Russian and foreign advisors, was one of the fruits of that Age of Enlightenment. In 1764 she bought in Berlin a magnificent collection of paintings for her new royal residence, the Winter Palace. It consisted of 225 canvases by Dutch and Flemish

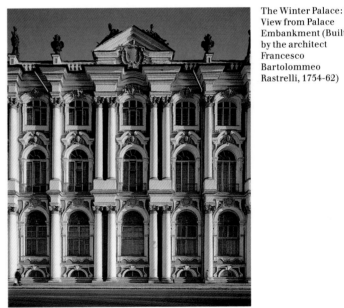

The Winter Palace: View from Palace Embankment (Built by the architect Francesco Bartolommeo Rastrelli, 1754-62)

masters which provided the nucleus of the Hermitage collection as we know it today.

Later still in the reign of Catherine II, three more palatial buildings were erected on the banks of the Neva to house the ever-growing Imperial collection. It came to be known as the Hermitage, in keeping with the fashion at royal courts throughout Europe for monarchs to seek refuge from the strict demands of court etiquette by relaxing in the company of their own intimate circle in private apartments filled with all manner of rare objects and works of art.

In the mid-nineteenth century, a special building, which came to be known as the New Hermitage, was erected to house the Museum's main collections. This was to be a public museum and was opened in 1852.

Today the State Hermitage Museum has a collection of almost three million exhibits representing the cultures and civilizations of many

7

Above
The Gallery of
Antique Paintings
(Built by the
architect Leo von
Klenze; designed by
George
Hiltenschperger;
1839-51)

Right
The Buildings of the
State Hermitage:
View from the river
Neva.

From right to left:
The Winter Palace
(Built by the
architect Francesco
Bartolommeo
Rastrelli, 1754-62)

The North Pavilion of
the Small Hermitage
(Built by the
architect Jean-
Baptiste Vallin de la
Mothe, 1767-69)

The Old (Large)
Hermitage (Built by
the architect Yury
Felten, 1771-87)

The Hermitage
Theatre (Built by the
architect Giacomo
Quarenghi, 1783-87)

nations and peoples, ranging from the Stone Age to the present day. This puts it on a footing with other great museums of the world such as the Louvre in Paris, the Metropolitan Museum of Art in New York and the British Museum in London.

The most valued asset of the Hermitage collection is without doubt its picture gallery: 50 rooms are taken up with the collection of French masters alone. Another 37 rooms house the Italian paintings and numerous others are filled with pictures from Dutch, Flemish, Spanish, German and other European schools.

A tour through the 353 rooms of the Hermitage brings the visitor face to face with great masterpieces of art – works by Raphael, Giorgione, Michelangelo, Leonardo da Vinci, Titian, Veronese, Rubens and many others whose art has enhanced the cultural history of mankind. It also enables the visitor to become acquainted with the history of Russian interior decoration, represented here by some of its finest creations.

The Hermitage, like the Louvre, is a museum with an all-embracing collection reflecting the achievements of the whole human race. Here are the monuments of Ancient Egypt, of the civilizations of Central Asia, Persia, China and the nomadic tribes of the Russian steppes, the masterpieces of Ancient Greece and Rome, of Byzantine as well as Russian culture, of French Impressionism and Post-Impressionism.

The State Hermitage Museum presents this book by way of an invitation to its galleries, where it is hoped all visitors will find much that is of interest. We are confident that the exhibits will provide a memorable experience and will be a source of delight both now and on future occasions.

Dr Vitaly Suslov

The Jordan (Main or Ambassadorial) Staircase of the Winter Palace (Built by the architect Francesco Bartolommeo Rastrelli, 1756-61)

After the Great Fire of 1837, the staircase was restored by Vasily Stasov.

The Treasures of the Hermitage

Good fortune is not as blind as it is generally thought to be. It is often nothing more than the result of sound, consistent actions that go unnoticed by the crowd, but which nevertheless make a particular event possible. Still more often it is the result of an individual's characteristics, nature and behaviour.' These are the words with which Catherine II, founder of the Hermitage, began her memoirs.

It was indeed a stroke of good fortune that led to her accession to the Russian throne. Whilst still a young, little-known German princess from the House of Anhalt-Zerbst, she was invited to Russia by the childless Empress Elizabeth, daughter of Peter the Great. On her conversion to the Russian Orthodox faith, the fifteen-year-old princess had been given the name Catherine (her German name was Sophia-Augusta). During this time she became engaged to her second cousin, who was to be chosen by Elizabeth as her successor, the future Peter III of Russia. In 1762, however, backed by the Guards, Catherine brought to an end the six-month reign of her husband and acceded to the throne herself. Like Peter the Great before her, Catherine was to prove herself worthy of such an honorific title. It was his superiority alone that she recognized, as testified by the inscription cut into the pedestal of the famous Bronze Horseman in St Petersburg: *Petro Primo Catharina Secunda.* Thus began a new era in Russian history.

With the accession of Catherine II, numerous reforms were inaugurated. New departures in the arts were undoubtedly the most remarkable, their purpose being the glorification of Catherine as an Enlightened Monarch. According to one historian's acute observation, 'her conduct always resembled that of an actress playing a part on stage.' Among these cultural enterprises was the establishment of a prestigious Imperial picture gallery, designed to challenge the most celebrated art collections of Europe. A general movement of reform and contact with Western culture had begun during the reign of Peter the Great, for it was he who first started to amass a personal art collection and who founded the Kunstkamera or Museum of Natural History, Russia's first public museum. Paintings were purchased for the decoration of palaces by his successors, and an Academy of Fine Arts was established, at first as a department of the St Petersburg Academy of Sciences and later as an independent institution. During the reign of Catherine II, the arts received a powerful new impetus as she began to promote private patronage as an aspect of state policy. The emergence of the Hermitage was part of this cultural renaissance.

*Left
Portrait of
Catherine II
(Fedor Rokotov,
c. 1770)*

*The Winter Palace:
The Great Church
(Edward Hau, mid-
19th century)*

The foundation of the Hermitage is traditionally dated to 1764, when the first acquisition – a collection of 225 paintings by Western European masters – was delivered to St Petersburg. Given her vast resources, Catherine II was able to secure most of the treasures that were offered to her, and when Frederick II of Prussia fell into financial difficulties and was unable to purchase the collection of paintings which the Berlin dealer Johann-Ernst Gotzkowsky had formed for him, Catherine bought it instead. The collection contained several masterpieces, including Frans Hals's *Portrait of a Young Man Holding a Glove.*

The Empress Catherine continued to take her art-collecting activities seriously, and this first purchase was followed by a number of successful acquisitions, made possible by the assistance of intermediaries such as Dmitry Golitsyn, Russian ambassador to Paris and The Hague, and the co-operation of renowned art connoisseurs such as Denis Diderot, François Tronchin, Frédéric-M. Grimm and many others, whose expertise helped to maintain the high quality of the collection.

In 1768 the private collections of the Prince de Ligne and Count Karl Coblentz were purchased in Brussels. The following year the collection of the late Count Heinrich von Brühl, a Dresden connoisseur who had been Chancellor to Augustus II, Elector of Saxony and King of Poland, became available and was acquired for the Museum, adding a number of Dutch and Flemish masterpieces to the collection. François Tronchin sold his private collection to the Empress in 1770, and in 1771 Prince Golitsyn acquired a number of Dutch paintings for the Museum at the sale of G. Braankamp's collection in Amsterdam. Unfortunately, they never reached their destination – St Petersburg – for the vessel with its valuable cargo sank in the Baltic Sea on its homeward voyage.

Further important acquisitions followed. In 1772, after long negotiations, the renowned collection of the French banker Baron Crozat, virtually complete, arrived from Paris. One of the most celebrated collections in France, it introduced to Russia the works of the great masters of the Italian Renaissance – Raphael's *Holy Family,* Giorgione's *Judith,* Titian's *Danäe* – together with priceless French, Dutch and Flemish works including Rubens's *Portrait of the Maid of Honour to the Archduchess Isabella* and Van Dyck's *Self-Portrait.* In 1779 the Hermitage collection was considerably enriched by the acquisition of paintings from one of the most outstanding collections in England, that of Sir Robert Walpole, Prime Minister to George I and George II, which

The Winter Palace: St George's Hall (Konstantin Ukhtomsky, 1862)

was acquired from his heirs. Finally, the last major addition to the holdings of the Hermitage during the eighteenth century came with the purchase in 1783 of the collection of Count Baudouin in Paris.

The Hermitage collections grew rapidly. The first catalogue, published in 1774, numbered over 2,000 canvases. Apart from the acquisitions of major collections, individual paintings, many of which are now internationally-recognised masterpieces, were purchased for the Museum from private sources and at auction. Catherine II also commissioned a number of celebrated artists to provide works expressly for the Russian collection. Thus, Boucher painted his *Pygmalion and Galatea* for St Petersburg's new Academy of Fine Arts; Chardin painted his famous *Attributes of the Arts* for the Conference Hall of the Academy (although this remained in the Hermitage); and Sir Joshua Reynolds painted his allegorical picture *The Infant Hercules strangling the Serpents*, which symbolized Russia's growing power.

Whilst the paintings comprise a considerable and significant part of the Hermitage collection, mention should certainly be made of Catherine's other acquisitions: collections of engravings; coins and medals; gemstones, her special passion; minerals (she was especially proud of her collection of minerals bought from the Academician Peter-Simon Pallace); and books, including the complete libraries of Diderot and Voltaire.

The Winter Palace: Gallery of 1812 (Edward Hau, 1862)

The fine art treasures amassed by Catherine II were originally accommodated in the rooms of the Winter Palace, the main residence of the Russian tsars, which was built on the banks of the river Neva in 1754-1762 to the designs of the architect Francesco Bartolommeo Rastrelli. As the collection grew, successive buildings were added: the Small Hermitage in 1764-1775, designed by Yury Felten and Jean-Baptiste Vallin de la Mothe; the Old (Large) Hermitage in 1771-1787, also designed by Yury Felten; and the Raphael Loggia, added onto the latter building alongside the Winter Canal, its first-floor gallery being a replica of the one painted by Raphael and his pupils in the Vatican Papal Palace.

As time went on, Catherine II turned instead to the theatre. The architect Giacomo Quarenghi was called upon to design the Hermitage Theatre, which was erected on the Winter Palace site in 1783-1787. The building was connected to the Old Hermitage by an arched bridge which spanned the Winter Canal. The rooms of the picture gallery now served both as reception rooms and theatre foyer, where parties of guests invited to Imperial performances were entertained.

'She [Catherine II] often invited me to dine with her and almost every day she permitted me to be present at the performance in the Hermitage,' recalled the French emissary, Count de Segur, in his memoirs. 'The appearance of this Hermitage did not fully correspond to its name, since on its threshold the beholder's eyes are struck by the enormous scale of its halls and galleries, the wealth of its furnishings and decoration, the multitude of paintings by Great Masters and by the pleasant "winter garden," whose green foliage, flowers and birdsong appear to have brought Italian springtime to the snowy North. The outstanding library seems to suggest that the Hermit of these halls prefers the illumination of philosophy to monastic privations. A history of the world in portraits is also to be found in a comprehensive collection of medals representing all races of mankind from all centuries.

'At the end of the palace is a beautiful theatre, a reproduction in miniature of the ancient theatre in Vicenza. It is semi-circular in shape: it has no boxes but rising tiers of seats arranged to

The New Hermitage:
First Room of
Modern Sculpture
(Luigi Premazzi,
1856)

form an amphitheatre. Twice a month the Empress invites the diplomatic corps here and those persons privileged to have access to the Court. On other occasions the number of spectators does not exceed a dozen.'

The personal art collection of Catherine II acquired the status of an Imperial museum in the reigns of her son Paul I and her grandson Alexander I who, taking advantage of the troubled situation in France in 1815, acquired several paintings from the Empress Josephine's gallery at Malmaison. This collection brought the Hermitage new works by Rembrandt, Rubens and Teniers the Younger. At about the same time, the first Spanish paintings were acquired for the Museum from the well-known collection of the Dutch banker, W. G. Coesvelt.

During the reign of Nicolas I, the Hermitage collections continued to expand. But in 1837 a tragedy occurred when fire broke out in the Winter Palace. It raged for three days, causing untold devastation, but thanks to the truly heroic efforts of those who fought the fire, the Hermitage building was saved, together with a considerable number of the Palace's priceless contents. Thousands of craftsmen participated in the restoration of the Palace, and its first rooms were completed in 1839.

In 1852, a major development in the history of the Imperial collection was inaugurated by Nicolas I when a new museum building was opened to the public. Called the New Hermitage, it had been built in 1839-1851 to designs by the Munich architect Leo von Klenze. The portico facing what used to be Millionnaya Street was adorned with ten huge atlantes, carved out of blocks of granite by the sculptor Alexander Terebenev. With the construction of the new

buildings, an up-to-date inventory and catalogue of the Museum's collections was carried out, a task made even more necessary by the Palace fire. For the first time Russian art was acknowledged with its own department, as were classical antiquities. The two galleries in the Small Hermitage, now left vacant, were to house the Romanov family portraits and the Memorial Collection of Peter I from the Kunstkamera, together with the collection of jewellery.

But Nicolas I is also associated with regrettable events in the history of the Hermitage for, as a result of his subjective decisions, many valuable pieces were to disappear from the Museum. A considerable number of masterpieces were sold, including Chardin's *Attributes of the Arts* and Lucas van Leyden's *The Healing of the Blind Man of Jericho*. Decades later, some of these works were recovered.

The mid-19th century saw a number of important acquisitions for the Hermitage including the collection of the Barbarigo Palace in Venice, which provided the Museum with some excellent paintings by Titian, several works from the collection of William II of The Netherlands, and classical antiquities from the collection of the Marchese Campana in Rome. These were followed by Leonardo da Vinci's *Madonna and Child*, purchased in 1865 from the Litta collection in Milan, and Raphael's *Madonna and Child*, bought from Count Conestabile in Florence in 1870. (This canvas was purchased originally for the Empress Maria Alexandrovna, who bequeathed it to the Hermitage in 1880.) In 1884 the Museum also acquired the collection of Anton Bazilevsky with its superb Oriental, Byzantine and medieval works of art, and a year later the collection of arms and armour from the Tsarkoye Selo armoury was added to its many treasures.

The Hermitage played a crucial part in the history of Russian art by acting as a valuable resource for young artists studying the Old Masters and by displaying the collection of Russian paintings, which was on view at the Hermitage from 1898. (This was to form the nucleus of the present Russian State Museum.)

Outstanding among the 20th-century acquisitions was the vast collection of Dutch and Flemish works that belonged to the well-known traveller and geographer Semenov Tien-Shansky, bought in 1910, and Leonardo da

The New Hermitage:
Voltaire's Library
(Konstantin
Ukhtomsky, 1859)

The fortunes of the Hermitage changed drastically in 1917. After the February Revolution it became known as the 'Ex-Imperial Hermitage.' Kerensky's Provisional Government ordered the art collection and all Palace property to be removed to Moscow, where it was to be stored in the Kremlin and in the History Museum in Red Square.

On the night of 25 October (Old Style) the Winter Palace, in which sessions of the Provisional Government had been held since the summer, was stormed by revolutionary forces. A few days later, Anatoly Lunacharsky, Commissar of the Soviet Government, declared the Winter Palace and the Hermitage state museums. (Eventually they were to be merged together to form the Hermitage we know today.)

At the end of 1920 the works of art that had been sent to Moscow were returned, but there now began a period when treasures were moved around the country to ensure their fair distribution among the different museums. For instance, in 1920 some 460 Old Masters were transferred to the State Museum of Fine Arts in Moscow alone. For its part, the Hermitage received part of Moscow's collection of Impressionist and Post-Impressionist works. New departments were established: Oriental arts and culture; the history of primitive civilizations; the history of Russian culture. The departments of Antiquities and Western European arts were completely rearranged. Archaeological excavations, initiated by B. Piotrovsky, brought to the Museum unique artefacts from the State of Urartu, one of the oldest Russian territories.

It was in many ways due to the shortsighted policies and the ignorance of Soviet foreign trade organizations, backed by the highest authorities, as well as a generally warped view of the role and significance of Russia's cultural heritage, that the Hermitage became increasingly involved in unprecedented sales of national treasures that could be justified neither on economic nor political grounds. The foreign trade organizations were undoubtedly spurred on by the fantastic number of works of art amassed during the short post-revolutionary period and the financial reward their sales seemed to promise. The efforts of the Hermitage staff to stem this destructive process met with little success. The catalogue of the auction held by the Rudolph Lepke Company in Berlin in 1931 lists an extensive and unique collection of objects of applied art and 108 paintings from the Stroganov Palace collection, including masterpieces by Van Dyck, Rubens, Rembrandt, Poussin and Boucher. The auction's commercial success was undermined by the mere fact that so many outstanding works of art were being sold off at the same time. Fortunately, in many cases bids did not reach the asking price and the works were later returned to the Hermitage.

Vinci's *Madonna with a Flower*, purchased from the Benois family collection and consequently known as the Benois Madonna.

The tragic year of 1914 marked the 150th anniversary of the Hermitage. Celebrations began with a performance at the Hermitage Theatre of a play written by Grand Prince Konstantin Konstantinovich, entitled *The King of the Jews*. In keeping with a tradition which started in the reign of Catherine II, the performance was followed by a dinner served in the rooms of the Hermitage. But such festivities were shortly to come to an end forever. World War I broke out in August that year and preparations began immediately for the evacuation of the Museum's contents. (However, only the treasures of the jewellery gallery were actually removed.)

During the Twenties and Thirties the Soviet Union found itself in a state of economic isolation. To stimulate business the Soviet Commissariat for Foreign Trade frequently offered works of art to foreign officials and businessmen for token sums. So it was that the US Ambassador to the Soviet Union Joseph Davis and his wife took advantage of these favourable terms when putting together their well-known collection of Russian art. Iraqi petroleum company chief Calouste Gulbenkian, US Minister of Finances Andrew Mellon, and others whose business was of particular interest to the Soviet Union, also unobtrusively acquired gems from the Hermitage. The scale of Andrew Mellon's 'deal' became evident when he presented Washington with twenty-one Hermitage paintings (which he had purchased for less than seven million dollars) to compensate for his failure to declare his profits to the US Department of Finances. These paintings became the core of the National Art Gallery in Washington: Van Eyck's *Annunciation*, Bot-

Top
The Pavilion Hall
(Edward Hau, mid-
19th century)

Above
The Winter Palace:
Moorish Hall
(Konstantin
Ukhtomsky, mid-
19th century)

all the treasures still in the Hermitage, which many of the Museum staff had lost their lives saving. In October 1945 the evacuated collections were returned to Leningrad and shortly afterwards the Hermitage was ready to receive its first post-war visitors. The restoration work, however, was to continue for many years to come.

Since the war the role of the Hermitage as an important research centre has expanded. Numerous archaeological expeditions, sponsored by the Museum and aimed at collecting Russian works of art, have been highly successful. Among the most valuable findings are frescoes from the ancient settlements of the area north of the Black Sea, from the medieval cities of Central Asia and the old Russian city of Pskov.

The past few years have been a period of great expansion for the Hermitage. A considerable number of works of art are purchased annually with state subsidies. Recent acquisitions have included a rare tapestry produced by a St Petersburg workshop in the 1730s; a miniature portrait of Catherine II; the dinner service manufactured on her orders for her favourite, Count Grigory Orlov; and Rastrelli's bust of Alexander Menshikov, the first Governor of St Petersburg. The Hermitage has also received generous gifts from citizens of the Soviet Union and friends from all over the world.

The Museum complex, too, has been augmented by a number of additional buildings: the palace of Alexander Menshikov is now devoted to the history of early 18th-century Russian culture and its relationship with Oriental and Western European cultures. The former General Headquarters of the Russian Army is to become a new museum of applied arts, and restoration work on the Hermitage Theatre is nearing completion: here, visitors will soon be able to see the excavated remains of the palaces of Peter I.

The exhibitions programme of the Hermitage is also growing, both in scope and in terms of international status. Along with the traditional exhibitions of new acquisitions each year, a number of monographic exhibitions are now arranged by the various departments. International exchanges of exhibitions and precious individual works of art are increasing, and the treasures of the Hermitage now travel all over the world.

Every year, thousands of visitors come to see the world-famous buildings of the Hermitage, and it is hoped that many more will have the opportunity to walk through this rich and wonderful museum and enjoy its countless magnificent treasures.

Dr Vladimir Matveyev

The Winter Palace: Rotunda
(Edward Hau, 1862)

ticelli's *Adoration of the Child*, Raphael's *Alba Madonna* and *St George* and Titian's *Venus with the Looking-Glass*, as well as masterpieces by Perugino, Veronese, Van Dyck, Frans Hals, Rembrandt and Velazquez. Numerous works of art originally from the Hermitage are now to be found in national and private collections the world over.

Only in 1934 did it become possible to stop these catastrophic sales. To the devastating list of losses one must add the book collection of the Winter Palace. The private library of Nicolas II, for example, was bought by the US Library of Congress.

On 22 June 1941 the Nazis attacked the Soviet Union, and the Museum staff, assisted by many volunteers, immediately began the second wartime evacuation of the Hermitage collection, this time to Sverdlovsk. More than two million items were sent off in two trains. The objects for the third train were in the process of being packed when the ring of the blockade closed. Thanks to the heroic efforts of the staff, both the collections and the buildings were saved. They continued with their research and even held scholarly conferences in the Museum buildings.

Towards the end of 1944, with the war still raging, a marvellous exhibition was mounted of

The Treasures

Head of a female elk
Bronze Age, 2,000 B.C.
Horn, length 19.5cm
From Yekaterinburg
(now Sverdlovsk) in
the Urals.

The Kostionki 'Venus'
Palaeolithic,
23,000 B.C.
Stone, height 10cm
From Kostionki,
Voronezh region.

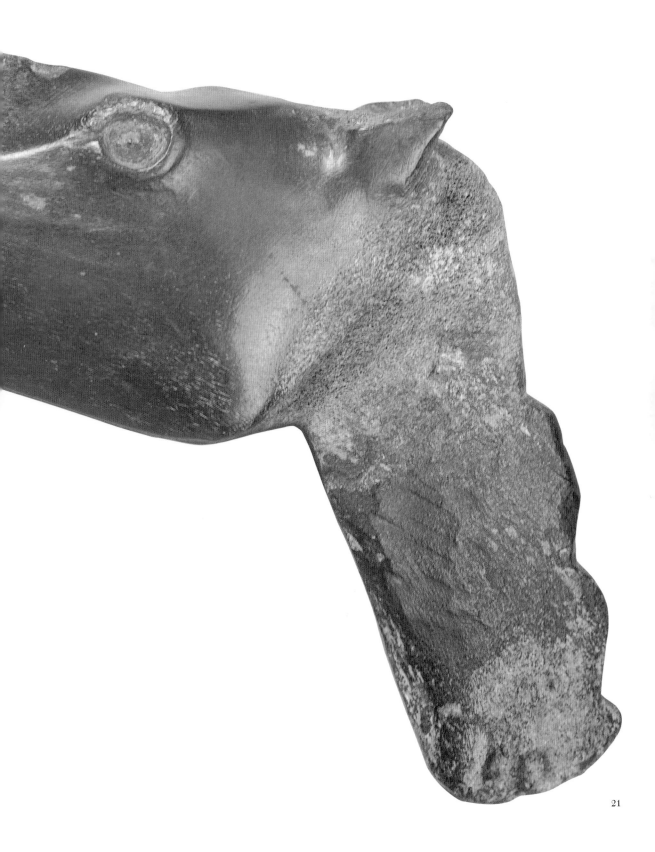

Fragment of the relief on the facing of the entrance to the tomb of the dignitary Merir-ankh End of Old Kingdom. Limestone, height 121cm. From Sakkara.

Statue of Amenemhat III Middle Kingdom, 19C B.C. Granite, height 86.5cm.

Comb
Late 5C-early 4C
B.C.
Gold, height 12.3cm
From Solokha burial
mound, Steppe, near
the Dnieper river.

Figure of a deer
7C-6C B.C.
Gold, length 31.5cm
From Kostromskaya
burial mound, N.
Caucasus.

Figure of a panther
7C-6C B.C.
Gold, height 10.8cm
Siberian collection
of Peter I.
From Altai.

*Pair of belt clasps
with three figures*
4C B.C.
Gold, height 13cm
Siberian collection
of Peter I.
From Altai.

*Quiver fitting for
bow and arrows*
4C B.C.
Gold, length 46.8cm
From Chertomlyk
burial mound,
Steppe, near the
Dnieper river.

Vase
4C B.C.
Gold, height 13cm
From Kul-Oba burial
mound, Kerch.

Amphora
Mid-4C B.C.
Silver and gilding,
height 70cm
From Chertomlyk
burial mound,
Steppe, near the
Dnieper river.

Rug
5C-4C B.C.
Wool, 200 x 185cm
From Pazyryk, 5th
burial mound, Altai.

Decorative figure of a mountain goat
7C-1C B.C.
Bronze, height
17.8cm
Tagar culture. From
Minusinsk basin,
Siberia.

Earring
4C B.C.
Gold, height 9cm
From Feodosian
necropolis, the
Crimea.

*Heracles Fighting the
Lion*
4C B.C.
Marble, height 65cm.
Roman copy of Greek
original.

*Mask of
Rhescuporis III*
3C.
Gold, height 22.5cm
From Bosporus.

The Gonzaga Cameo
3C B.C.
Sardonyx, 15.7 x
11.8cm
From Alexandria.

*Icon of St Grigorii
the Miracle-Worker*
12C.
Tempera on wood,
81 x 53cm
Acquired from the
State Russian
Museum in
Leningrad, 1935.

*Diptych depicting
circus scenes*
5C.
Ivory, height 33cm
Acquired from A. P.
Bazilievsky's
collection in Paris,
1885.

*Christ – The Good
Shepherd*
5C.
Marble, height
68.5cm
Found in the ruins of
a church in the
village of Chinga,
near Pandern in
Vifaniya (Asia
Minor); acquired in
1915.

*Dish of Bishop
Paternus*
Late 5C-early 6C
Silver, diameter
61cm
Found in a burial
mound in the village
of Malaya
Pereshchepino,
Poltara Gubernia,
1912; acquired in
1914.

Left
SIMONE MARTINI
c.1284-1344
*The Virgin of
the Annunciation*

Tempera on wood
(half of diptych),
30.5 x 21.5cm
Bequeathed by
Count Stroganov in
Rome, 1911.

Above
GIAMBATTISTA
CIMA DA
CONEGLIANO
1459-1517
The Annunciation
1495

Tempera and oil on
canvas (transferred
from wood),
136.5 x 107cm
Transferred from the
Golitsyn Museum in
Moscow, 1886.

ANNIBALE
CARRACCI
1560-1609
*Holy Women at the
Tomb of Christ*
Late 1590s
Oil on canvas,
121 x 145.5cm
Acquired from the
Coesvelt collection
in London, 1836.

UGOLINO
LORENZETTI
Active 1320-48
The Crucifixion
Mid 14C
Tempera on wood,
91.5 x 55.5cm
Acquired from the
collection of Prince
Gagarin in Petrograd
(via the State
Museum Fund) in
1919.

PAOLO VERONESE
1528-1588
Pietà
1576-82
Oil on canvas,
147 x 111.5cm
Acquired from the
collection of Baron
Crozat de Thiers in
Paris, 1772.

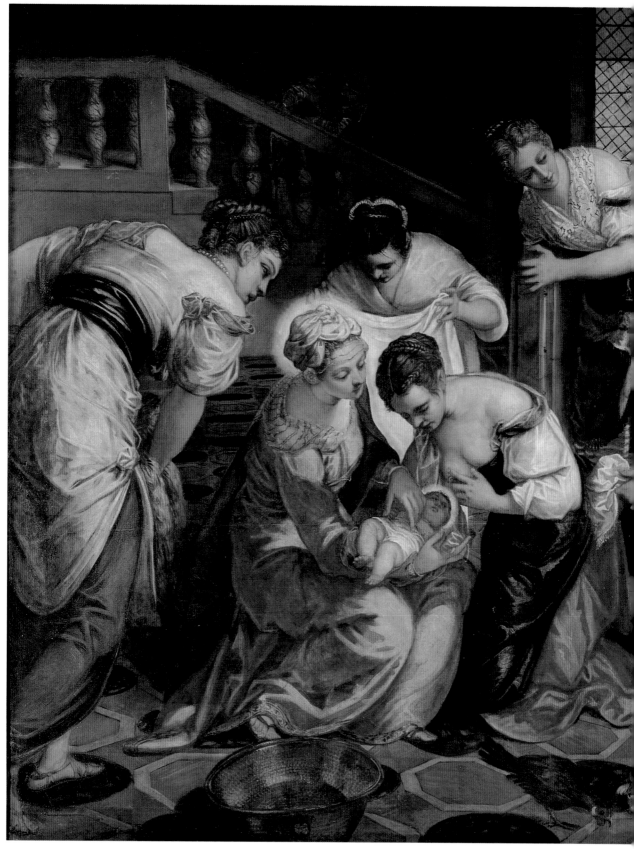

JACOPO ROBUSTI
TINTORETTO
1518-1594
The Birth of John the Baptist
c.1550
Oil on canvas,
181 x 266cm
Acquired from the
collection of Baron
Crozat de Thiers in
Paris, 1772.

Right
TITIAN
(Tiziano Vecellio)
1485/1490-1576
St Sebastian
c.1570
Oil on canvas,
210 x 115cm
Acquired from the
Barbarigo collection
in Venice, 1850.

Far right
PERUGINO
(Pietro Vannucci)
c.1450-1523
St Sebastian
c.1495
Tempera on wood,
53.5 x 39.5cm
Acquired from the
collection of the
Marchese Campana
in Rome in 1910;
previously in the
collection of
Princess
Volkonskaya.

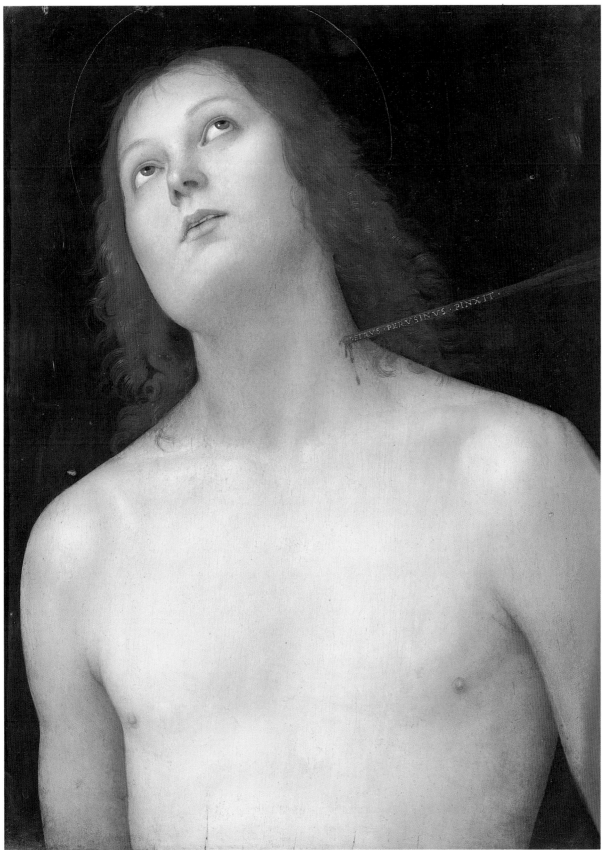

LEONARDO
DA VINCI
1452-1519
*Madonna and Child
(Litta Madonna)*
Late 1470s-c.1490/91
Tempera on canvas
(transferred from
wood), 42 x 33cm
Acquired from the
collection of Duke
Litta in Milan, 1865.

RAPHAEL
(Raffaello Santi)
1483-1520
*Madonna and Child
(Conestabile
Madonna)*
Late 1502-early 1503
Tempera on canvas
(transferred from
wood), 17.5 x 18cm
Acquired from Count
Conestabile della
Staffa in Perugia
1870; given to the
Hermitage in 1881.

ANTONIO
ROSSELLINO
1427-1479
Madonna and Child
Mid 15C
Marble, 67 x 54cm

FRA ANGELICO
1386/1387-1455
*Virgin and Child
with St Dominic and
St Thomas Aquinas*
1424-30

47

PONTORMO
(Jacopo Carucci)
1494-1557
*Madonna and Child
with St Joseph and
St John the Baptist*
Late 1521-early 1522
Oil on canvas,
120 x 98.5cm
Acquired from the
collection of Countess
Mordvinova in
Petrograd, 1923 (via
the State Museum
Fund).

RAPHAEL
1483-1520
*Holy Family with
beardless St Joseph*
1506
Oil and tempera on
canvas (transferred
from wood),
72.5 x 57cm
Acquired from the
collection of Baron
Crozat de Thiers in
Paris, 1772.

LUCA GIORDANO
1632-1705
The Forge of Vulcan
Oil on canvas (trans-
ferred from wood),
192.5 x 151.5cm

Acquired from the
Walpole collection at
Houghton Hall,
England, 1779.

MICHELANGELO
BUONARROTI
1475-1564
Crouching Boy
Early 1530s
Marble, height 54cm

CARAVAGGIO
(Michelangelo
Merisi da
Caravaggio)
1571-1610
Youth with a Lute
c.1595
Oil on canvas,
94 x 119cm
Acquired from the
Giustiniani
Collection, Rome,
1808.

EL GRECO
(Domenikos
Theotocopoulos)
1541-1614
*Apostles Peter and
Paul*
1587-92

Oil on canvas,
121.5 x 105cm
Gift from P.P.
Durnovo in St
Petersburg, 1911.

JOSE DE RIBERA
1591-1652
St Onufri
1637
Oil on canvas,
130 x 104cm
Entered the
collection before
1859.

FRANCISCO DE
ZURBARÀN
1598-1664
St Lawrence
1636
Oil on canvas,
292 x 225cm
Acquired from the
collection of
Maréchal Soulte, in
Paris, 1852.

DIEGO
VELÁZQUEZ
1599-1660
The Breakfast
1618
Oil on canvas,
108.5 x 102cm
Entered the
collection between
1763 and 1774.

ANTONIO DE
PEREDA Y SALGADO
1608-1678
Still Life
c.1652
Oil on canvas,
80 x 94cm
Acquired from the
Coesvelt collection
in Amsterdam, 1814.

BARTOLOMÉ
ESTEBAN
MURILLO
1617-1682
*Assumption of the
Virgin*
1670s
Oil on canvas,
195.5 x 145cm
Acquired from the
Walpole collection at
Houghton Hall,
England, 1779.

ROBERT CAMPIN
(The Master of
Flémalle)
c.1380-1444
*Madonna by the
Fireside*
1430s
Oil on wood (half
of diptych),
34 x 24.5cm
Bequeathed by D.P.
Tatischev in St
Petersburg, 1845.

JAN BRUEGHEL
1568-1625
Forest Landscape
(Rest on the way to
Egypt)
1607

Oil on wood,
51.5 x 91.5cm
Acquired from the
Brühl Collection,
Dresden, 1769.

FRANS SNYDERS
1579-1657
*The Fishmonger's
Stall*
Oil on canvas,
209.5 x 341cm
Acquired from the
collection of Baron
Crozat de Thiers in
Paris, 1772.

DAVID TENIERS
the YOUNGER
1610-1690
*Monkeys in the
Kitchen*
Oil on canvas
(transferred from
wood), 36 x 50.5cm
Acquired from the
collection of the
Empress Josephine
at the Château de
Malmaison near
Paris, 1815; in 1806 it
had been taken from
the collection of the
Landgrave von
Hessel-Kassel by
Napoleon.

PIETER PAUL
RUBENS
1577-1640
The Carters
c.1630
Oil on canvas
(transferred from
wood), 86 x 126.5cm
Acquired from the
Walpole collection at
Houghton Hall,
England, 1779;
formerly part of
Cardinal Mazarin's
collection in Paris.

Left
ANTHONY
VAN DYCK
1599-1641
Family Portrait
Late 1621
Oil on canvas,
113.5 x 93.5cm
Entered the
collection before
1774; prior to 1770 in
the collection of
Lalive de Julie in
Paris.

Right
ANTHONY
VAN DYCK
1599-1641
Self-Portrait
Late 1620s-early
1630s
Oil on canvas,
116.5 x 93.5cm
Acquired from the
collection of Baron
Crozat de Thiers in
Paris, 1772.

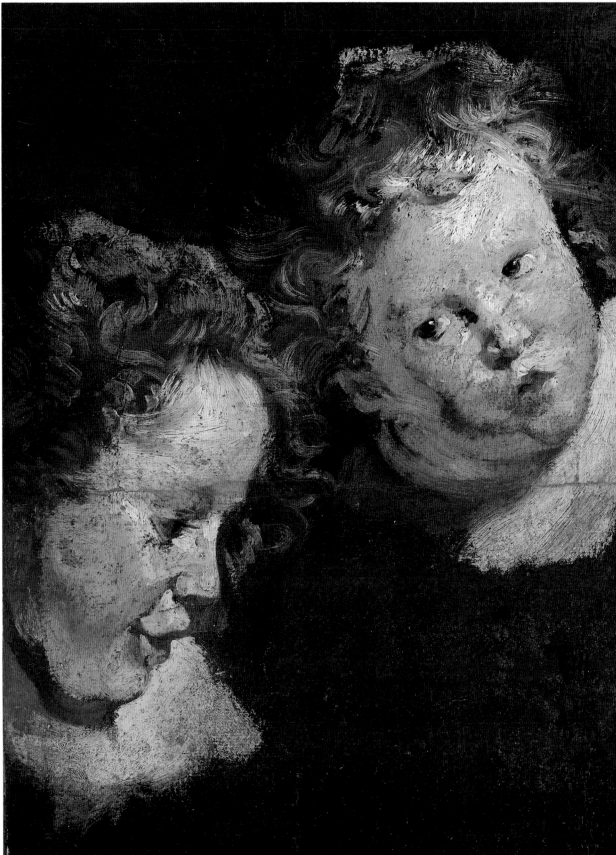

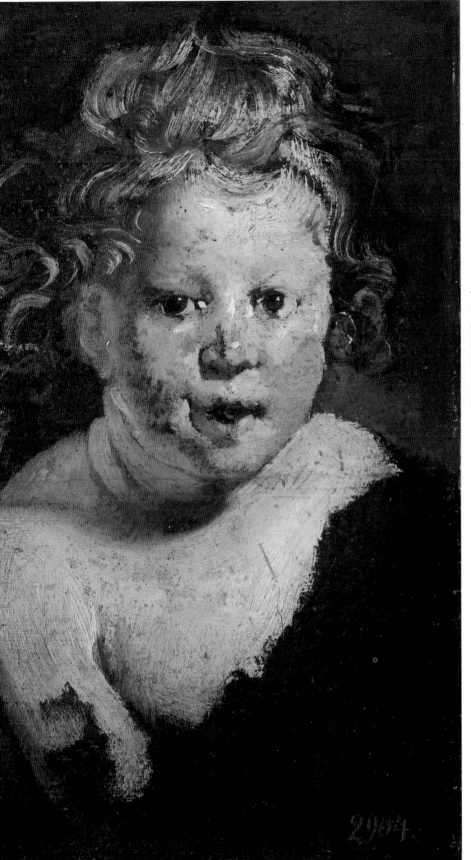

JACOB JORDAENS
1593-1678
*Three Children's
Heads*
c.1618
Oil on canvas
(transferred from
paper glued onto
wood), 42.5 x 53.5cm
Entered the
collection between
1763 and 1774.

PIETER PAUL
RUBENS
1577-1640
*Perseus and
Andromeda*
Early 1620s
Oil on canvas
(transferred from
wood), 99.5 x 139cm
Acquired from the
collection of Count
von Brühl in
Dresden, 1769.

PIETER JANSSENS
ELINGA
1623-1682
*Room in a Dutch
House*
Oil on canvas,
61.5 x 59cm
Acquired from the
collection of P.P.
Stroganov in St
Petersburg, 1912.

WILLEM CLAESZ
HEDA
1594-1680/1682
Breakfast of Crab
1648
Oil on canvas,
118 x 118cm
Made over from the
State Museum Fund,
1920.

GERRIT (Gerard)
VAN HONTHORST
1590-1656
Childhood of Christ
c.1620
Oil on canvas,
137 x 185cm
Gift from P.P.
Durnovo in
Leningrad, 1925 (via
the State Museum
Fund).

FRANS HALS
1581/1585-1666
*Portrait of a Young
Man Holding a Glove*
c.1650

Oil on canvas,
80 x 66.5cm
Acquired from the
collection of J.E.
Gotzkowsky in
Berlin, 1764.

REMBRANDT
HARMENSZ
VAN RIJN
1606-1669
*Portrait of an
Old Jew*

1654
Oil on canvas,
109 x 85cm
Acquired from the
Baudouin collection
in Paris, 1781.

Left
REMBRANDT
HARMENSZ
VAN RIJN
1606-1669
The Return of the Prodigal Son
c.1668/1669
Oil on canvas,
262 x 205cm (on the right and lower edge of the painting there are additions 10 cm wide)
Acquired by D.A. Golitsyn from the collection of the Duc d'Amézune in Paris, 1776.

Above
REMBRANDT
HARMENSZ
VAN RIJN
1606-1669
David's Farewell to Jonathan
1642
Oil on wood,
73 x 61.5cm
Acquired for Peter I from the collection of Jan van Beiningen in Amsterdam, 1716; transferred to the Hermitage from the Monplaisir Palace in Peterhof near St Petersburg in 1882.

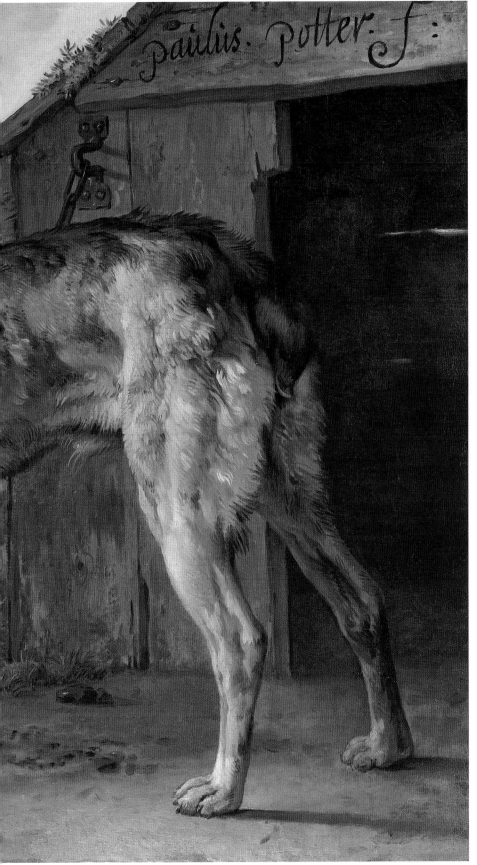

PAULUS POTTER
1625-1654
Chained Dog
Oil on canvas,
96.5 x 132cm
Acquired from the
collection of the
Empress Josephine
at the Château de
Malmaison near
Paris, 1814.

FRANS JANSZ
VAN MIERIS I
1635-1681
*Morning of a
Young Lady*
1659-60
Oil on wood,
51.5 x 39.5cm
Acquired from the
collection of Count
von Brühl, Dresden,
1769.

Above
GERARD
TERBORCH
1617-1681
Glass of Lemonade
Oil on canvas
(transferred from
wood), 67 x 54cm
Acquired from the
collection of the
Empress Josephine
at the Château de
Malmaison near
Paris, 1814.

Right
GABRIEL METSU
1629-1667
Breakfast
c.1660
Oil on wood,
56 x 42cm
Acquired from the
collection of the
Empress Josephine
at the Château de
Malmaison near
Paris, 1814.

DIRCK VAN
BABUREN
c.1595-1624
Concert
c.1623
Oil on canvas,
99 x 130cm
Acquired from the
collection of J.E.
Gotzkowsky in
Berlin, 1764.

Above
ANTON RAPHAEL
MENGS
1728-1779
Self-Portrait

Oil on wood,
102 x 77cm
Entered the
collection between
1774 and 1783.

Right
AMBROSIUS
HOLBEIN
c.1495-c.1519
*Portrait of a
Young Man*

1518
Oil on wood,
44 x 32.5cm
Entered the
collection between
1774 and 1783.

LUCAS CRANACH
the ELDER
1472-1553
Venus and Cupid
1509
Oil on canvas
(transferred from
wood), 213 x 102cm
Entered the
collection between
1763 and 1774.

LUCAS CRANACH
the YOUNGER
1515-1586
*Christ and the Fallen
Woman*
Oil on copper
(transferred from

wood), 84 x 123cm
Transferred from the
Museum of the
Academy of Fine Arts
in St Petersburg in
1920; acquired by the
Academy in 1762.

Figurine of a knife grinder
Early 18C
Silver, diamonds, rubies, emeralds, pearls, coral, enamel, glass; height 8.8cm
Dresden.

CASPAR DAVID FRIEDRICH
1774-1840
On Board a Sailing Ship
Oil on canvas, 71 x 56cm
Transferred from the 'Cottage' Palace-Museum in Peterhof near Leningrad, 1958.

THOMAS
GAINSBOROUGH
1727-1788
*Portrait of a Lady in
Blue*
Late 1770s

Oil on canvas,
76 x 64cm
Bequeathed by A.Z.
Khitrovo in
Petrograd, 1912/
1916.

GEORGE DAWE
1781-1829
Portrait of General
Alexei Yermolov
Before 1824
Oil on canvas,
70 x 62.5cm
Painted to hang in
the Military Gallery
of the Winter Palace.

SIR JOSHUA
REYNOLDS
1723-1792
*Cupid unfastens the
Belt of Venus*
1788
Oil on canvas,
127.5 x 101cm
Acquired from the
collection of G.A.
Potemkin, 1792.

SIR JOSHUA
REYNOLDS
1723-1792
*The Infant Hercules
strangling the
Serpents sent by Hera*
1786-88
(commissioned from
the artist in 1785)
Oil on canvas,
303 x 297cm
Acquired from the
artist, 1789.

Overleaf
NICOLAS POUSSIN
1594-1665
*Moses bringing forth
Water from the Rock*
1649
Oil on canvas,
123.5 x 193cm
Acquired from the
Walpole collection at
Houghton Hall,
England, 1779.

JEAN-HONORÉ
FRAGONARD
1732-1806
The Stolen Kiss
Late 1780s
Oil on canvas,
45 x 55cm
Transferred from the
Laziensky Palace in
Warsaw, 1895.

ANTOINE WATTEAU
1684-1721
*An Embarrassing
Proposal*
c.1716
Oil on canvas,
65 x 84.5cm
Acquired from the
collection of Count
von Brühl in
Dresden, 1769.

CLAUDE LORRAIN
(Claude Gellée)
1600-1682
*Midday or The Rest on
the Flight into Egypt*
1651 or 1661
Oil on canvas,
113 x 157cm
Acquired from the
collection of the
Empress Josephine
at the Château de
Malmaison near
Paris, 1815; taken
from the Landgrave
von Hessen-Kassel
collection.

HYACINTHE RIGAUD
1659-1743
Portrait of a Scholar
Oil on canvas,
80 x 65cm
From the Myatlev
collection in
Petrograd, 1922.

JEAN-LOUIS VOILLE
1744-after 1804
*Portrait of Baroness
Stroganova*
1781-82
Oil on canvas,
86 x 68.5cm
Transferred via the
State Museum Fund
from the collection
of D.G. Ginzburg in
Petrograd, 1919.

ELISABETH-
LOUISE VIGÉE
LEBRUN
1755-1842
Self-Portrait
1800
Oil on canvas,
78.5 x 68cm
Donated by the artist
to St Petersburg's
Academy of Fine Arts
in 1800; transferred
from the Museum of
the Academy of Fine
Arts, 1922.

JEAN-ANTOINE
HOUDON
1741-1828
Bust of Voltaire
1778
Marble, height 69cm

JEAN-BAPTISTE
SIMÉON CHARDIN
1699-1779
*The Attributes of
the Arts*
1766
Oil on canvas,
112 x 140.5cm
Painted for St
Petersburg's
Academy of Fine Arts
and in the Hermitage
collection since
1766; sold at an
auction in 1854;
re-entered the
collection via the
Commission for the
Improvement of
Children's Lives in
Leningrad, 1926.

FRANÇOIS
BOUCHER
1703-1770
*Pygmalion and
Galatea*
1767
Oil on canvas,
234 x 400cm
Donated by the artist
to St Petersburg's
Academy of Fine Arts
in 1766 and brought
to St Petersburg by
E.M. Falconet;
transferred from the
Museum of the
Academy of Arts in
Petrograd, 1922.

*Mantelpiece clock
'Cupid and Psyche'*
From the Pierre-
Philippe Thomire
workshops in Paris,
1799
Gilded bronze and
patina, marble,
height 85cm.

JEAN-BAPTISTE
GREUZE
1725-1805
*Portrait of Count
Stroganov as a Child*
1778
Oil on canvas,
50 x 40cm
Transferred from the
Stroganov Palace
Museum in
Leningrad, 1923.

ANTOINE WATTEAU
1684-1721
*Actors from a French
Theatre*
c.1712

Oil on wood,
20 x 25cm
Acquired from the
collection of Baron
Crozat de Thiers in
Paris, 1772.

JEAN-BAPTISTE
GREUZE
1725-1805
*The Paralytic or The
Fruits of a Good
Education*
1763
Oil on canvas,
115.5 x 145cm
Acquired from the
artist, 1766.

THEODORE
ROUSSEAU
1812-1867
Market in Normandy
1830s
Oil on wood,
29.5 x 38cm
Transferred from the
Museum of the
Academy of Arts in
Petrograd, 1922;
formerly part of the
collection of the
Kushelev Gallery.

BARON ANTOINE
JEAN GROS
1771-1835
Napoleon Bonaparte
on Arcole Bridge
Copy of a picture

painted in 1797
Oil on canvas,
134 x 104cm
Transferred from the
collection of N.N.
Leichtenbergsky in

Leningrad, 1924 (via
the State Museum
Fund).

JEAN AUGUSTE
DOMINIQUE
INGRES
1780-1867
*Portrait of Count
Guriev*
1821

Oil on canvas,
107 x 86cm
Transferred from the
collection of A.N.
Naryshkina in
Petrograd, 1922 (via
the State Museum
Fund).

CHARLES FRANÇOIS
DAUBIGNY
1817-1878
*Banks of the
River Oise*
Oil on canvas,
25.5 x 41cm
Acquired from
O. Ovsyanikova in
Petrograd, 1919.

JEAN-BAPTISTE
CAMILLE COROT
1796-1875
*Trees in a Marshy
Landscape*
1855-60

Oil on canvas,
25.5 x 38cm
Transferred from the
collection of A.M.
Somov in Petrograd,
1922 (via the State
Museum Fund).

JEAN LÉON
GERÔME
1824-1904
*Duel after a Masked
Ball*
1857
Oil on canvas,
68 x 99cm
Transferred from the
Museum of the
Academy of Arts in
Petrograd, 1922;
formerly part of the
collection of the
Kushelev Gallery.

Above
FERDINAND
VICTOR EUGÈNE
DELACROIX
1798-1863
*A Moroccan Saddling
his Horse*
1855
Oil on canvas,
56 x 47cm
Transferred from the
Museum of the
Academy of Arts in
Petrograd, 1922;
formerly part of the
collection of the
Kushelev Gallery.

Right
FERDINAND
VICTOR EUGÈNE
DELACROIX
1798-1863
*Lion Hunt in
Morocco*
1854
Oil on canvas,
74 x 92cm
Transferred from the
Museum of the
Academy of Arts in
Petrograd, 1922;
formerly part of the
collection of the
Kushelev Gallery.

Left
HENRI ROUSSEAU
1844-1910
*In a Tropical Forest:
Fight between a
Tiger and a Bull*
1908(?)
Oil on canvas,
46 x 55cm
Transferred from the
State Museum of
New Western Art in
Moscow, 1930;
formerly part of S.I.
Shchukin collection
in Moscow.

Above
PIERRE BONNARD
1867-1947
*Early Spring
(Little Fauns)*
1909
Oil on canvas,
102.5 x 125cm
Transferred from the
State Museum of
New Western Art in
Moscow, 1948;
formerly part of the
I.A. Morozov
collection in
Moscow.

VINCENT VAN GOGH
1853-1890
Cottages
1890
Oil on canvas,
60 x 73cm
Transferred from the
State Museum of
New Western Art in
Moscow, 1948;
formerly part of the
I.A. Morozov
collection in
Moscow.

CLAUDE OSCAR
MONET
1840-1926
Haystack in Giverny
1886
Oil on canvas,
61 x 81cm
Transferred from the
State Museum of
New Western Art in
Moscow, 1931;
formerly part of the
S.I. Shchukin
collection in
Moscow.

ANDRÉ DERAIN
1880-1954
The Port of Le Havre
c.1905/6
Oil on canvas,
59 x 73cm

Transferred from the
State Museum of
New Western Art in
Moscow, 1930;
formerly part of the
S.I. Shchukin
collection in
Moscow.

ALBERT MARQUET
1875-1947
The Bay of Naples
1909
Oil on canvas,
61.5 x 80cm
Transferred from the
State Museum of
New Western Art in
Moscow, 1948;
formerly part of I.A.
Morozov collection
in Moscow.

HENRI MATISSE
1869-1954
View of Collioure
1906
Oil on canvas,
59.5 x 73cm
Transferred from the
State Museum of
New Western Art in
Moscow, 1948;
formerly part of the
S.I. Shchukin
collection in
Moscow.

HENRI EDMOND
CROSS (Delacroix)
1856-1910
*The Church of Santa
Maria degli Angeli
near Assisi*
1909
Oil on canvas,
74 x 92cm
Transferred from the
State Museum of
New Western Art in
Moscow, 1948;
formerly part of the
S.I. Shchukin
collection in
Moscow.

MAURICE DE
VLAMINCK
1876-1958
*Small Town on a
Lake Shore*
c.1907
Oil on canvas,
80 x 99cm
Transferred from the
State Museum of
New Western Art in
Moscow, 1948;
formerly part of the
S.I. Shchukin
collection in
Moscow.

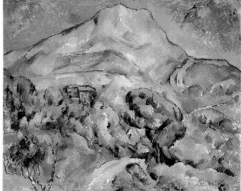

Top
CAMILLE PISSARRO
1830-1903
*Place du Théâtre
Français, Paris*
1898
Oil on canvas,
65.5 x 81.5cm
Transferred from the
State Museum of
New Western Art in
Moscow, 1930;
formerly part of the
S.I. Shchukin
collection in
Moscow.

Above
PAUL CÉZANNE
1839-1906
Mont St Victoire
1900
Oil on canvas,
78 x 99cm
Transferred from the
State Museum of
New Western Art in
Moscow, 1948;
formerly part of the
I.A. Morozov
collection in
Moscow.

Right
PABLO PICASSO
1881-1973
The Dance of the Veils
1907
Oil on canvas,
150 x 100cm
Transferred from the
State Museum of
New Western Art in
Moscow, 1948;
formerly part of the
S.I. Shchukin
collection in
Moscow.

Far right
CORNELIS
THEODORUS
MARIE VAN
DONGEN (known as
Kees)
1877-1968
Red Dancer
c.1907
Oil on canvas,
99 x 80cm
Transferred from the
State Museum of
New Western Art in
Moscow, 1948;
formerly part of the
N.P. Ryabushinsky
collection in
Moscow.

Épreuve d'artiste

Overleaf
PAUL CÉZANNE
1839-1906
*Girl at the Piano
(Ouverture to
'Tannhäuser')*
c.1868/69
Oil on canvas. 57 x
92 cm. Transferred
from the State
Museum of New
Western Art in
Moscow, 1948; before
that part of the I.A.
Morozov collection
in Moscow.

PABLO PICASSO
1881-1973
*Dance with
Banderillas*
1954
Lithograph,
47.5 x 63.8cm
Gift from D.H.
Kahnweiler, Paris,
1967.

AUGUSTE RODIN
1840-1917
Poet and Muse
1905
Marble, height 61cm.

Right
PIERRE AUGUSTE
RENOIR
1841-1919
*Portrait of the Artist
Jeanne Samary*
1878
Oil on canvas,
173 x 103cm
Transferred from the
State Museum of
New Western Art in
Moscow, 1948;
formerly part of the
M.A. Morozov
collection in
Moscow.

Far right
PAUL GAUGUIN
1848-1903
*Woman Holding a
Fruit*
1893
Oil on canvas,
92 x 73cm
Transferred from the
State Museum of
New Western Art in
Moscow, 1948;
formerly part of I.A.
Morozov's collection
in Moscow.

EMILE ANTOINE
BOURDELLE
1861-1929
*Beethoven (Large
Tragic Mask)*
Bronze, height 76cm
Presented by the
artist's daughter,
1972.

PABLO PICASSO
1881-1973
*The Absinthe
Drinker*
1901
Oil on canvas,
73 x 54cm
Transferred from the
State Museum of
New Western Art in
Moscow, 1948;
formerly part of the
S.I. Shchukin
collection in
Moscow.

HENRI MATISSE
1869-1954
Conversation
1909
Oil on canvas,
177 x 217 cm
Transferred from the
State Museum of
New Western Art in
Moscow, 1930;
formerly part of the
S.I. Shchukin
collection in
Moscow.

Above
ÉDOUARD
VUILLARD
1868-1940
*Indoor Scene with
Children*
1909
Tempera on
cardboard, pasted on
canvas, 84 x 73cm
Transferred from the
State Museum of
New Western Art in
Moscow, 1930;
formerly part of the
Zeitlin collection,
Moscow.

HENRI MATISSE
1869-1954
Music
1910
Oil on canvas,
260 x 389cm
Transferred from the
State Museum of
New Western Art in
Moscow, 1948;
formerly part of the
S.I. Shchukin
collection in
Moscow.

Left
PABLO PICASSO
1881-1973
*Two Sisters
(The Visit)*
1902
Oil on canvas, glued
on wood,

152 x 100cm
Transferred from the
State Museum of
New Western Art in
Moscow, 1948;
formerly part of the
S.I. Shchukin
collection in
Moscow.

Above
FERNAND LÉGER
1881-1955
Composition
1924
Oil on canvas,
73 x 92cm
Transferred from the

State Museum of
New Western Art in
Moscow, 1948;
originally donated by
B.N. Ternovetz, 1927.

145

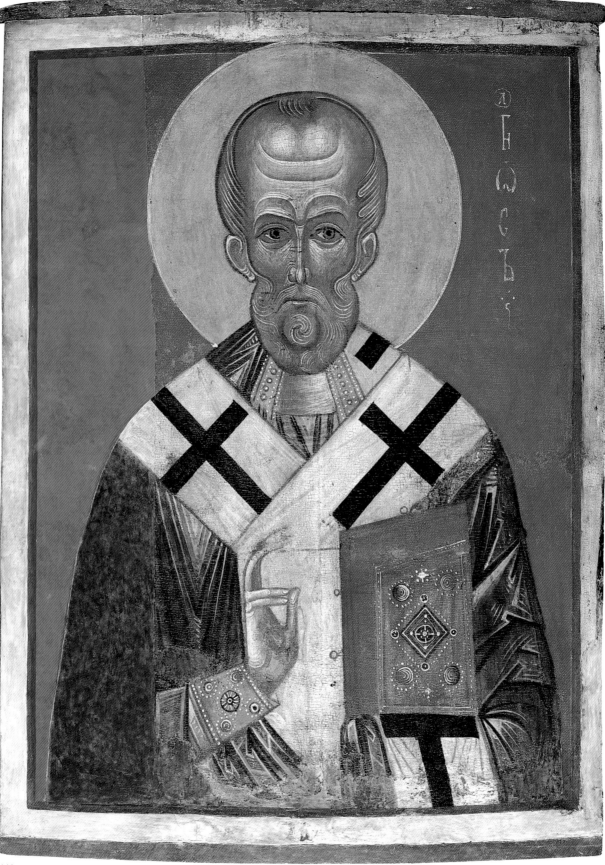

Icon of St Nicolas
13C-early 14C
Tempera on wood,
107 x 79.3cm
Novgorod School.

Icon of Our Lady
15C-early 16C
Tempera on wood,
158.5 x 60.5cm
Moscow School.

*Plaque depicting the
Mother of God*
12C–13C
Gold, enamel;
3.8 x 3.0cm
Fragment of diadem.
From Kiev.

NEKTARII
KULIUKSIN
*Icon of John the
Theologian in Silence*
1679
Tempera on wood,
109 x 85cm
From Kyrill-
Belozersky
monastery.

GRIGORII S.
MUSIKIYSKY
1670/1671-after 1739
*Portrait of Peter the
Great in front of the
Fortress of SS Peter
and Paul*
1723
Gold, enamel;
6.5 x 8.8cm

GRIGORII S.
MUSIKIYSKY
1670/71-after 1739
*Portrait of Catherine I
in front of
Ekaterinhov*
1724
Gold, enamel;
6.5 x 8.8cm

BARTOLOMEO
CARLO RASTRELLI
1675-1744
*Bust of A.D.
Menshikov*
1716-17
Bronze, height
122.5cm.

*Sun dials and bas-
relief*
Late 1710s-early
1720s
Ivory, wood;
27cm, 21.5cm, 5.5cm
Made by Peter the
Great.

Goblet – ship
1706
Silver, height 37cm
Moscow(?)

*Carnival sleigh with
the figure of
St George*
Mid 18C
Wood, gold-leaf;
length 360 cm

*Dish with the
monogram of
Catherine II*
1762
Silver, 59 x 46cm
Craftsmen Andrei
Gerassimov and
Aleksei Polozov,
Moscow.

*Items from the
Service of Empress
Elizabeth Petrovna*
1756
Porcelain and gilt;
spoon: length 18.6cm;
plate: diameter
24.5cm; sugar bowl:
length 28.4cm; salt
dish: length 11cm
Imperial Porcelain
Works, St Petersburg.

*Items from the Orlov
Service*
1740s
Porcelain, gilt and
silver; cream jug:
height 6cm; bowl:
length 17.2cm; dish:
diameter 23.4cm;

rouge box: height
5.6cm; teapot: height
19.7cm
Imperial Porcelain
Works, St Petersburg.

CARL-LUDWIG
CHRISTINEK
1732/33-1792/94
*Portrait of Aleksei
Bobrinsky as a Child*
1769
Oil on canvas,
90 x 73.5cm
Transferred from the
State Museum of
Ethnography, 1941;
formerly in the
Bobrinsky collection
in St Petersburg.

IVAN VISHNYAKOV
1699-1761
*Portrait of Stepanida
Yakovleva*
After 1756
Oil on canvas,
90 x 72cm
Transferred from the
State Museum of
Ethnography, 1941;
formerly in Yakovlev
collection in
St Petersburg.

ALEKSEI ANTROPOV
1716-1795
*Portrait of Father
Fyodor Dubyansky*
1761
Oil on canvas,
99.5 x 76.5cm
Transferred from
N.A. Sidorov
collection in
Leningrad, 1932.

Samovar
1896
Gilded copper, gold,
ivory; height 54cm
Workshop of Vasiliy
Batashov. Tula.

Urn
1873
Jasper, height 130cm
From Yekaterinburg
stoneworks, Urals.

Snuff-box
Mid 18C
Gold, silver,
diamonds, sapphire,
7.4 x 5.5 x 2.6cm
Craftsman Jérémie
Pauzié.

Vanity chest and mirror
c.1801
Steel, blue steel, gilded bronze, glass; height 70cm
From Tula; made for the Empress Maria Feodorovna, wife of Emperor Paul I; part of the main Hermitage collection.

Drop-front writing-desk
Mid 18C
Ivory, wood; height 54.5cm
From the village of Kholmogori, Arkhangelsk Gubernia.

Dresser
c.1910
Oak, brass, stained
glass; height 260cm
Workshop of
H. Rosenburg,
St Petersburg.

Right
Miniature replicas of the Imperial regalia (the grand Imperial crown, the smaller Imperial crown, orb and sceptre), on marble pedestal
End 19C
Silver, gold, diamonds, sapphires, rubies; large crown: height 7.3cm; small crown: height 3.8cm; orb: height 6.8cm; sceptre: length 15.8cm
Workshop of Peter Carl Fabergé. The original regalia is in the Hall of Diamonds in the Kremlin, Moscow.

Far right
Cornflowers and ears of corn
1880s
Gold, diamonds, rock crystal, enamel; height 29cm
Workshop of Peter Carl Fabergé.

Floor Plans

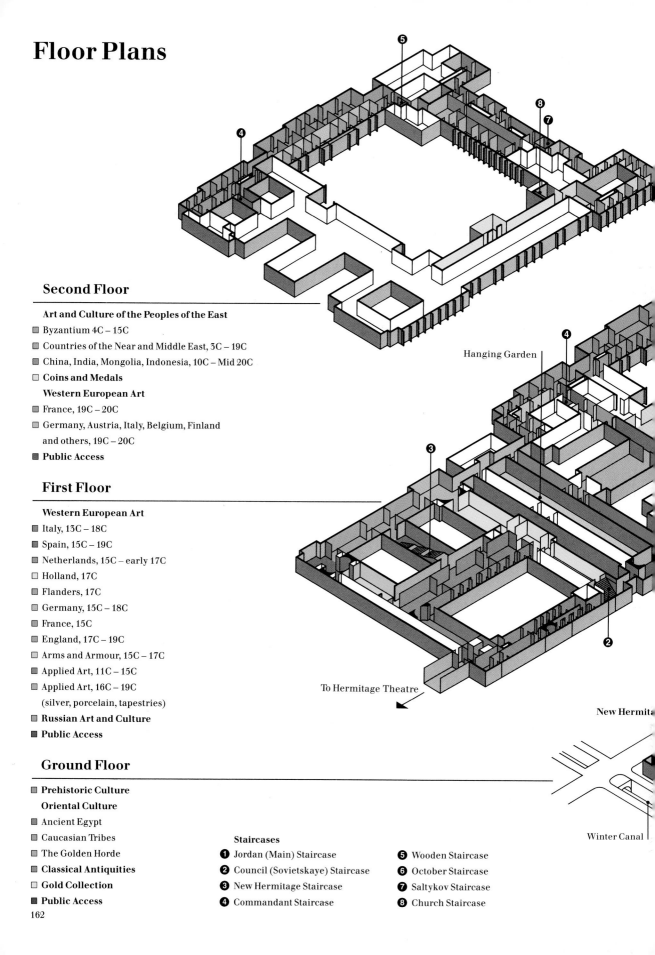

Second Floor

Art and Culture of the Peoples of the East
- Byzantium 4C – 15C
- Countries of the Near and Middle East, 3C – 19C
- China, India, Mongolia, Indonesia, 10C – Mid 20C
- Coins and Medals

Western European Art
- France, 19C – 20C
- Germany, Austria, Italy, Belgium, Finland
  and others, 19C – 20C
- **Public Access**

First Floor

Western European Art
- Italy, 13C – 18C
- Spain, 15C – 19C
- Netherlands, 15C – early 17C
- Holland, 17C
- Flanders, 17C
- Germany, 15C – 18C
- France, 15C
- England, 17C – 19C
- Arms and Armour, 15C – 17C
- Applied Art, 11C – 15C
- Applied Art, 16C – 19C
  (silver, porcelain, tapestries)
- **Russian Art and Culture**
- **Public Access**

Ground Floor

- **Prehistoric Culture**
- **Oriental Culture**
- Ancient Egypt
- Caucasian Tribes
- The Golden Horde
- **Classical Antiquities**
- Gold Collection
- **Public Access**

162

Hanging Garden

To Hermitage Theatre

New Hermit

Winter Canal

Staircases
1. Jordan (Main) Staircase
2. Council (Sovietskaye) Staircase
3. New Hermitage Staircase
4. Commandant Staircase
5. Wooden Staircase
6. October Staircase
7. Saltykov Staircase
8. Church Staircase

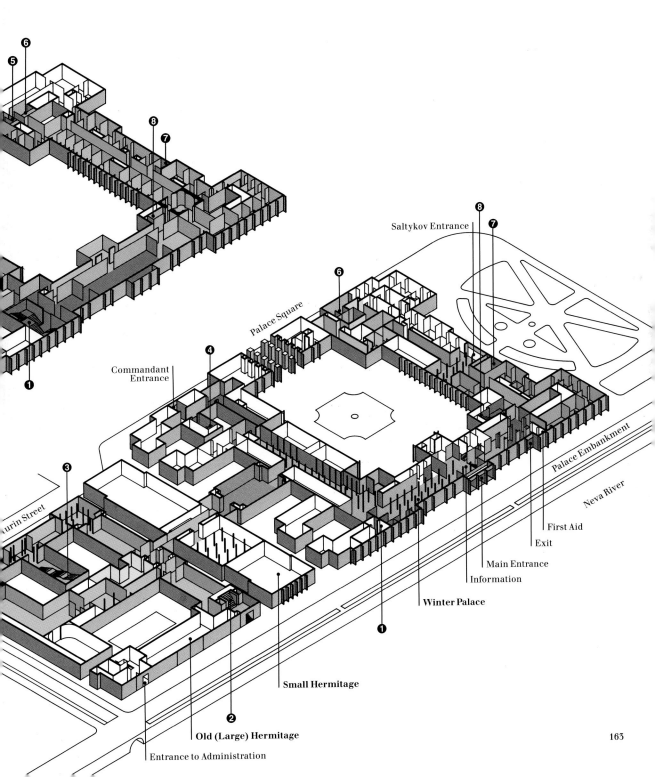

Saltykov Entrance

Palace Square

Commandant
Entrance

Palace Embankment

Neva River

...urin Street

First Aid

Exit

Main Entrance

Information

Winter Palace

Small Hermitage

Old (Large) Hermitage

Entrance to Administration

Index